I0060786

SUCCESS!

Grit, Guts
& Integrity

Brick Tower Press
Habent Sua Fata Libelli

MENTOR
BUSINESS BOOKS

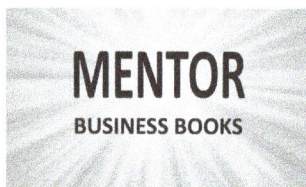

Brick Tower Press
Manhanset House
Shelter Island Hts., New York 11965-0342
Tel: 212-427-7139
bricktower@aol.com • www.BrickTowerPress.com

All rights reserved under the International and Pan-American Copyright Conventions. No part of this publication may be reproduced, stored in a retrieval system, or transmitted in any form or by any means, electronic, or otherwise, without the prior written permission of the copyright holder.
The Brick Tower Press colophon is a registered trademark of J. T. Colby & Company, Inc.

Library of Congress Cataloging-in-Publication Data
Perry, Marjorie A.
Success!—Grit, Guts & Intregrity
p. cm.

1. Business & Economics—Women in Business.
2. Business & Economics—Leadership.
3. Business & Economics—Small Business.
4. Biography & Autobiography—Cultural, Ethnic & Regional—African-American & Black.
Nonfiction, I. Title.

ISBN: 978-1-955036-77-1, Trade Paper

Copyright © 2024 by Marjorie A. Perry
December 2024

SUCCESS!
—Grit, Guts & Integrity

Marjorie A. Perry

This book is dedicated to the next generation of up and coming entrepreneurs, may your journey to serve others gives even greater success!

Table of Contents

Preface

"I first met Marjorie over lunch at a restaurant in Newark. I was trying to entice her to join the board of the New Jersey Symphony. She was a ball of energy, a font of wisdom and a raconteur. She was perfect for the Symphony—but little did I know she was also the perfect mentor for me.

Marjorie Perry's story is not just one of her own personal triumphs, but a testament to the resilience and determination required to navigate the intricate landscape of entrepreneurship. Her experiences resonate with the fundamental truths about the struggles and victories faced by those who dare to dream, act upon those dreams and take control of their destiny. Marjorie's journey is a vivid illustration of how grit—the relentless pursuit of goals despite the obstacles—can propel one to unprecedented heights.

As you delve into *Success!—Grit, Guts & Integrity*, you will be drawn into a narrative that is as compelling as it is educational. Marjorie's insights into leadership, perseverance, and ethical conduct are invaluable for anyone seeking to make a meaningful impact in their professional (and even personal) lives. Her story serves as a powerful reminder that true success is not measured solely by financial gains or accolades, but by the strength of character and the positive influence one has on others.

It takes an industry titan to achieve what Marjorie has. It takes a wise human to acknowledge when they have stumbled.

It takes a true leader to share what they have learned through it all. My hope for you, dear reader, is that through *Success!—Grit, Guts & Integrity* you too get to experience joy, inspiration, and mentorship that I have from my friendship with Marjorie. "

—*Gabriel van Aalst*
   President and CEO, New Jersey Symphony and
   Marjorie Perry Super Fan

"Excellent book. Marjorie Perry is a trailblazer. She is someone who has never shied away from challenges or allowed obstacles to prevent her from accomplishing her goals, no matter how lofty the aspiration or how difficult the journey. Marjorie's talent, intelligence and tenacity have enabled her to achieve incredible success in a field where African-American women are dramatically underrepresented and have, historically, faced many barriers to entry, especially at the highest levels. In this book, she shares incredibly valuable insights related to her experiences and the lessons she learned en route to becoming a leader and a mentor. Marjorie's thoughts on self-belief and self-awareness are prescient. Her willingness to embrace uncertainty and not be deterred by the possibility of failure provides an example for those with an entrepreneurial spirit. Additionally, her commitment to leading while reaching back to create opportunities for those who follow is inspirational. We are proud to call her an alumna and friend of NJIT, and we are grateful for all she has done for our university and our students."

—*Dr. Teik C. Lim, Pres. NJIT*

"While having a fascinating life, the life's lessons from this humble yet successful business woman is a valuable reminder of the importance of giving back. Marjorie's never ending commitment to family, friends and family is a testament to her passion for always doing what is right. The impact she has had on countless diverse student interns has created our entrepreneurs of the future. Her amazing story is one that many should know and most certainly aspire to."

—Robert Cohen
   President, Stryker's Digital, Robotics and Enabling Technologies

Foreword

Marjorie Perry is an extraordinary leader and an even better person. I've known Marjorie for over 20 years. She is a trailblazer. She is tenacious. She has a big heart, but she is also tough as nails. She would have to be to be a successful businesswoman in a mostly male-dominated world of construction.

Let's be more specific. It's been incredibly challenging to be an African American woman competing and succeeding in a largely white, male-dominated, industry—but that's what Marjorie has done. Look in the dictionary under the word grit and you will find a picture of Marjorie. She is all about grit.

What you will read in this book is her story of not just how to succeed, but also the times she came up short when things didn't work out the way she had hoped. But, like most great leaders, Marjorie learned every step of the way from those experiences.

As someone who writes, teaches, and coaches about leadership (and sometimes struggles as a leader), I know a great leader when I see one, and that is who Marjorie Perry is. But she is also a natural born teacher and coach, which is primarily why she wrote this book, *Success!—Grit, Guts & Integrity*. It's not enough for Marjorie to be successful and make money (who can argue with that?). But she also wants to share her experiences and the lessons she has learned with others. Why? Because she has always wanted to make a difference, not just for herself and for her company but for those she touches. Like the best leaders—Marjorie Perry has a big heart and pays it forward.

Let me also disclose that Marjorie is the chair of the board of our non-profit media production company, the Caucus Educational Corporation. In that capacity, Marjorie has been an invaluable resource for me as the President of our organization. She has always told me the way it is and what I needed to hear as opposed to simply telling me what I may have wanted to hear. That's what a friend does. They tell you the way they see it and don't sugar coat it in the process.

Marjorie's book doesn't sugar coat it. She tells you exactly the way she sees it and I'm betting that for those fortunate enough to read her book, you will be better for it. You will learn, be inspired and be motivated to overcome whatever challenge you are facing in business and in life. That's what Marjorie Perry has done. She has overcome obstacles. Like me, Marjorie was born and raised in Newark, NJ. There is a reason we call Newark "Brick City."

Marjorie has fought the fight in the arena and picked one of the toughest industries to compete in and she is playing at the highest level. That's not easy. But as Marjorie Perry knows and she shares in this book, nothing in business (or life) is ever easy, which is why when you succeed, it is that much sweeter. Congratulations, my friend. You have written a powerful and impactful book and I've learned so much from reading it and I know others will as well. So, start turning the pages and you will quickly understand and see what I mean.

—Steve Adubato, Ph.D., is an Emmy Award-winning broadcaster, author and leadership coach.

Prologue

Dear Braveheart,

My path has not always been smooth. I've had to learn many lessons (often by making mistakes first) in order to persevere and become the successful businesswoman I am today. I want to share some of those lessons to help you steer clear of the rocky parts and pitfalls as you pursue your dream. For example, I've learned on my journey of self-discovery that every good *business* lesson also contains a *life* lesson. When we learn these life lessons, we develop not only our external wealth, but also what I call our "internal wealth." You can take this to the bank: The mindset required to construct a business – the inner resources needed to take an idea from start, to start-up, to success – are the same resources that will serve you well whatever path you take in life.

This book is your invitation to embark on the most wonderful adventure of your life – to strike out on a path toward establishing your independence and start your own business. To persevere. I am going to guide you, step-by-step, so that you can do your own thing, build your business, and avoid some of the costly mistakes that I made on my path to making millions. I hope, that as you read this book, you will develop an attitude of abundant thinking and that you will be empowered to transition from being an employee/manager to becoming the leader/owner you desire to be as I lead you on this journey.

So, sit back and enjoy the story as I share how I, an inner-city kid and a woman of color, learned to play in a sandbox where many people would not expect to see someone like me. I thank you for giving me the opportunity to light the way and inspire you to begin your own wonderful adventure.

Chapter 1

Who Am I to Give You Advice?

How do you know if you have the right stuff, the right know-how, or the right background to take a good idea or opportunity and turn it into your "little economic engine that can?" What I've discovered is that there is no one right answer, no single path, no upbringing, and no one-size-fits-all model that will guarantee to turn out a successful innovator every time. There is, however, a right formula and a right approach. If you look at my life, you can understand that where you start your journey does not dictate where you end up. The important part is what you do in order to get from Point A to Point B.

I grew up in Newark, New Jersey and attended Newark's public schools. Today, that community and those schools are often unfairly associated with failure. In my day, the schools I attended – South Eighth Street School and Barringer High School in the city's North Ward – were among the best. Former U.S. Congressmen, the late U.S. Supreme Court Justice, William

J. Brennan, Jr., composer Jerome Kern, and poet Amiri Baraka were among its alumni.

I liked school and my teachers liked me. Some of them took me home on weekends and during summer vacation days to play with their children. They exposed me to a world far beyond that of my own neighborhood through outings to Lincoln Center or other New York City venues. If they lived in Newark, they lived either in the Vailsburg section or the North Ward (both lovely areas and mainly white), or they lived in one of Essex County's affluent suburbs, like Livingston or West Orange.

Most of my teachers had married well, many to lawyers or doctors or other successful professionals. As a result, they also lived very well; they had swimming pools in their backyards and employed housekeepers to clean and gardeners to handle their lush grassy lawns. When my feet hit the hard concrete that was my backyard, I knew my life was very different from theirs. They had full kitchens and huge dining rooms, while my home contained one small table pushed against the wall of our little kitchen. I began to dream about what my life could be like if I studied hard and got a good education. Could I achieve a life like theirs?

"You can do it," they told me.

I believed them.

Most of our neighbors owned their homes, as well. The fact that my parents owned our home helped shape me; I grew up in a community knowing that it was important to "own your own."

During this time, Newark was coping with the effects of the 1967 riots that encompassed the city for five days as a response to police mistreatment of members of the African American community. There were 26 killed, over 700 injured, and millions of dollars in damages done. [1] As the city recovered, Newark was

---

1. "Five Days of Unrest That Shaped, and Haunted, Newark" *The New York Times.*
https://www.nytimes.com/2017/07/11/nyregion/newark-riots-50-years.html

left with a reputation that was less than sterling, as well as a thriving, politically engaged populace.

My neighborhood was not a failing neighborhood. It was rich with people who knew each other, who believed in getting involved with each other and who desired to work to make things better. There was always some meet-the-candidate political tea on our block, NAACP meetings, and people who encouraged all of us children to reach for our dreams.

My mother was extremely involved in these types of activities, and she was the one who inspired my passion for serving. She was big on giving back, and always found ways to do so, from participating in the Girl Scouts, to attending PTA meetings, or just making sure others' voices were heard. She wanted to make a difference and seeing her do that was empowering and inspiring to me.

My father had graduated from high school in Nutley, New Jersey — a blue collar to middle class, predominately white town. For an African American (Negro was the label of the times) man to grow up in that kind of community and go to that kind of school back in the '40s was a big deal, given the fact that he was raised in the era of segregation. You didn't have to be in the South to experience discrimination.

For better or worse, my father's high school experience must have had a lot to do with shaping the man he became. He was an intelligent man and an avid reader who worked as a computer programmer for Blue Cross Blue Shield in the late '50s and early '60s. That meant he was a pioneer. It was a time when not every workplace welcomed a Black man who wasn't holding a broom or cleaning the floors.

He was not a talkative man, nor was he a kind caring individual. He was a stern disciplinarian, and I was a rebellious child. He was full of criticism of me and seldom offered me any type of encouragement. Mostly, he seemed angry about something, perhaps the opportunities he'd missed out on in life. Meanwhile, my mother had her hands full raising three girls, including my younger sister, who was disabled. My mother was loving but often silent. Neither of my parents thought I needed to go to college. Instead, they expected me to go to work right out of high school, then get married and have kids. Fortunately, from early on, I had other ideas.

Still, my father did transmit some important values to me. I learned from him, sometimes through his words, and more often from the way he lived his life. He showed up for work every day. *"Do your job. Finish what you start. Be responsible."* Those words – his words – have guided me through my life, and most certainly as a businesswoman. His words have stood the test of time, and as you will see, helped push me toward success and allowed me to survive disaster.

"Do your job. Finish what you start. Be responsible."

Those were some of the things that shaped me. What are the things that have shaped you? And what is it that incubates and forms successful entrepreneurs?

Bill Gates, the founder of Microsoft®, came from a wealthy family whose deep roots encompassed banking, law, and education. We might expect success when a person grows up in that kind of environment, but consider this: John D. Rockefeller, founder of Standard Oil and the richest man in the world during his lifetime, had a father who was a "pitch man." Some might call his father a con artist because he sold a $25 "cure" for cancer. Or what about Madam C.J. Walker, an African American woman and self-made millionaire from hair care products who was born to former slaves? She was orphaned by age seven and was forced to work in the cotton fields as a child to survive.

Some entrepreneurs inherit a family business. They experience a life of ease and plenty and can fall back on their family history of enterprise and innovation. Others grow up with adversity. Neither a history of living through hard times, nor having experienced a well-to-do upbringing will predict your potential for success. In the end, it will come down to who YOU are, not who your daddy or mommy were.

There is no scientific data to confirm the best background or set of experiences which ensure that you become a successful entrepreneur. In my experience, successful entrepreneurs are shaped by a sense of tenacity that propels them to complete what they start. They don't give up, nor are they thrown off by rejection or criticism. They can even be stubborn, or let's say, "focused," when it comes to their goals.

True entrepreneurs will not be deterred from their dreams. It wouldn't be surprising to hear a burgeoning entrepreneur say that they're going to do what they think is best going to get them to their goals, despite conventional advice or wisdom.

"Money is not the true measure of how successful your dream is."

By the way, that goal or dream cannot just be about making money. If the idea is *just* to make money, you've already failed before you begin. *Money is not the true measure of how successful your dream is.* You've got to be clear on this distinction; it is key to not only love what you do, but also have a guiding purpose — a reason *why* you do what you do that is truly, deeply fulfilling. Otherwise, you may as well not do it at all.

The money will come and go. The only people who have a steady stream of income are employees. If you want a paycheck every two weeks, I recommend that you get a job. That is one of the points I'm going to repeat more than once because it's an important point to understand. If you're an entrepreneur, you must be prepared for the ebbs and flows of the life you are creating for yourself. There are lots of reasons other than making money which drive people to go into business. In my case, I wanted to build wealth, yes, but I also craved independence.

I also found the idea of putting people to work very appealing. Employing people was, for me, another way to give back to my community. I knew this would come further down the line, but I also didn't think being a solo entrepreneur was the right path for me. Hiring people, then making payroll each month and therefore enabling them to support themselves and their families, was an incredibly fulfilling element of the journey. It was a fantastic, tangible sign of growth for me once I got there. It would be tough work, but I knew the impact that a thriving business could have on my clients and employees, as well as myself.

I had no one to educate me about business. I did have an uncle who had a trucking company, and I'm sure his insights would have come in handy, but the elders in my family did not talk to the children in ways which passed on their wisdom. The idea that I could work for myself, or how to go about it, was completely foreign to me. These were certainly not the pieces of advice I'd ever heard around the family dinner table. In truth, I really didn't get any kind of advice or much encouragement from my family to be the best "me" I could be.

But thankfully, there were always those other voices in my ear that told me I could do the things I dreamed of doing. Yes, there were scarier voices there, too. Those voices would ask what I, an African American woman, thought she was doing going into the construction business. Those voices called me an impostor. And maybe they had a point, but I didn't let those voices drown out the happy ones.

The happy voices inside me reminded me that I always wanted to be something more. They pushed me to show everyone (including myself) what I was truly capable of. They encouraged me not to let them see me sweat, just let them see what I could accomplish. And those were the voices I paid attention to.

You must also learn to listen to the right voices. For example, I have benefited from the fact that experienced people — some at the top in their fields — have talked to me along the way, from my teachers early on, to my co-workers and clients and colleagues.

But most of the time, it is the uplifting voice inside of you that deserves your utter and complete attention. In the days when I worked in corporate America, I found it hard to fit into the corporate mold. Consistently, my inner voice told me a nine-to-five job was not going to cut it.

So, just as I saw the kind of homes and lifestyles that others enjoyed when I was a child, I believed that I could have those things as well. In my mind, these desires were totally reachable as long as I worked hard. I put myself through college, working and learning. Attending college gave me a sense of independence and convinced me that I could work my way through, or into, anything as long as I set my mind to it and maintained the right attitude.

"Learn from your failures and avoid future mistakes."

I want to tell you that if you work toward success, you will sometimes fail. But if you fail forward and move on —learn from your failures and embrace what you need to know to avoid some future mistakes — you will succeed.

I am a successful woman and a powerful person. I deliver on million-dollar contracts. Success is why I have been interviewed on television, written up in magazines and newspapers, and have been named one of the most influential women in the country. Success is why I sit on the dais and speak from the podium.

My construction company, MZM, moves the earth to make way for big buildings. We move the sand to replenish beaches. We build. We haul. MZM puts people to work. The little girl from the Central Ward grew up to build a company that does all that and more.

But you also need to hear about the stumbles, the mistakes that taught me as much as the degrees, certifications, and kudos I've earned. You need to hear about how I've persevered.

I, Marjorie A. Perry, CEO, small business owner and entrepreneur, am my greatest "construction project." And I assure you that if you go into business for yourself, you will be your greatest project as well.

Chapter 2

Playing the Game

The Super Bowl! It's an event that holds not just the nation's attention, but also that of the world. Super Bowl 2014 was held on my home turf at MetLife Stadium in East Rutherford, New Jersey. This was the first time in years that a stadium without a dome in the northeast had been picked to host the Super Bowl.

My company won the contract for snow removal at the stadium on Super Bowl weekend. I want to use this experience as the starting point to help you to understand what any small business will face and must take into consideration when a contract is awarded, or a new client comes on board.

By 2014, my business was thriving. I had survived a $1 million mistake I made some years ago when I was too proud and naive to do the things I will be telling you to do shortly. By the time Super Bowl 2014 rolled around, MZM was back on solid footing, with contracts approaching $20 million in revenues. Believe me, you don't get to play in the business end of the Super Bowl unless you convince the Powers-That-Be that you are among the best. And my contract was to handle one of the most critical needs of this particular Super Bowl.

From the moment MetLife Stadium got the nod, skeptics criticized the decision, saying there was too much at risk; bad weather could ruin the National Football League's premier event. Additionally, months before the 2014 Super Bowl was played, the venerable *Farmer's Almanac* prophesied "biting cold and stormy weather" for Super Bowl Sunday.

If this prophecy came to pass, the job of clearing the stadium walkways and seats would be MZM's responsibility, and the world's cameras would be there to show the entire country how well that job was done.

It turned out the almanac was right. More than eight inches of snow pelted the New York/New Jersey region. But fortunately, the snow started six hours *after* the whistle blew on the last Super Bowl play. The storm sat on the region for hours, pummeling New Jersey with inclement weather. What would it have meant for MZM if that storm had arrived earlier? Could we have handled that size job in a very short amount of time, knowing that it's this kind of situation that can make or break a company and its reputation?

Could we have handled it? Actually, yes. With forethought, I had recruited 250 people, all of whom had pledged to answer my call anytime on Super Bowl weekend if so much as one snowflake fell. Months in advance, we'd organized everything down to having a fleet of buses on standby to move our workers to the site if need be.

Less than two weeks before the big day, Mother Nature provided a dress rehearsal, dumping nearly a foot of snow on the region. We called in the troops and contacted 85 workers, 50 of whom answered. You always need a cushion, and we had one. We transported the work crew to the stadium, where they cleared snow from the walkways and ramps inside the stadium, then shoveled the snow into many trucks that carted it away. We also cleared and polished every seat in MetLife stadium, dry as a bone, all in timely fashion. The MZM machine cranked up and worked well, even though I was sitting at my desk in California that day. That's preparation. That's organization. That's what any small business needs. Our guys were even featured in a TV news report about Super Bowl preparedness. It was a good day.

It would, of course, have been a vastly different scenario if the snow had come when the teams, the media, and more than 82,000 fans were eagerly streaming into MetLife Stadium. The logistics would have been even more complicated, but I know we had the organization in place to handle whatever the weather dished out.

That's not to say that as well prepared and organized as you might be, you don't go a little crazy and sprout a few extra grey hairs when you must deal with a high visibility, no-room-for-error contract, particularly when a factor as uncontrollable as the weather dictates your moves.

There were a lot of good reasons to go for such a contract, and for MZM, money was not at the top of the list. Being involved with the Super Bowl was great for branding MZM. It is good to have your name high up in the atmosphere like that. Good publicity is like money in the bank when it comes to bringing in future business.

Time is money, however, and we put in a lot of prep work starting months before the big day. MZM had to recruit people, and because everyone had to pass the FBI and Homeland Security clearances, we went through six times the applications to pick out 250 finalists even though we were only obligated to provide 100 workers at most. The extra people were insurance; we had to make sure that enough of them would clear the background checks. Also, some of those on our list had part-time jobs elsewhere while others did not. Given the long timeline between preparation and execution, we could not be sure how many would be available to answer the call if it snowed during

Super Bowl weekend. When all was said and done and every person, truck, bus, and equipment rental had been paid, there was not actually much profit from all that work.

Under our contract with the stadium, we only got paid when we worked, and that big snowstorm came *after* our contracted time. So, we got only one payday from that snow just before the Super Bowl. Other small businesses that were awarded the contracts to provide official souvenirs, for example, likely made out better.

Sometimes a lot of work and not much profit are part of life for a small business. You have to choose what business you go after. But as I said, money was not our chief consideration in going after this contract.

What I remember most was how enthusiastic our guys were about being able to work at MetLife Stadium to clear the snow. For the majority, it was their first time in the place, and they were excited to be part of the Super Bowl, if only in a tangential way. And I was happy to put people to work. A lot of the guys who signed on were unemployed, but that day, they made $19 an hour and got to work for eight hours. At the time, minimum wage in New Jersey was $8.25, so we got to offer these guys more than twice the rate they may have expected elsewhere. That's one of the truly wonderful things about running a business; you get to give somebody a payday.

Chapter 3

Know Who You Are

Answer the question, "Who am I?" This the first step to building a business, and you would do well to take a good long pause to ponder it before you read further.

For any entrepreneur or small business owner, who you are matters more than almost any other factor. I'm not talking about the "you" at the superficial level that you present to your boss and co-workers. Your family and friends may not even know about that inner, more private you that you need to probe to decide whether your business idea is solid —if you have the proverbial right stuff to be the driving force behind an organization.

Should you ignore the warnings about the risks being too big? Should you turn your back on the well-meaning advice of others who don't support your dreams, but who are encouraging you to keep your "good" job and benefits? Who you are will determine whether the discouraging words you will most likely hear from your family and friends are true wisdom or barriers between you and a dream that is achievable.

Once you begin this journey, you will be your business and your business will be you. You will be linked in a relationship like no other. You are embracing an entity that will be more demanding than any spouse or child. This thing you create will take your money, obliterate your vacation plans, destroy your sleep, and test all of your other relationships.

So, the first task is to be clear on who you are, what you want, and what you are truly willing to risk. The first step requires a deep-down reality check. Take this warning seriously: Know who you are and what you are willing to stand for. Lie to yourself on this initial self-check and you will regret it.

It's easy to find other kinds of self-tests and quizzes that claim to tell you whether or not you have the right stuff. I recently took a 25-question Small Business Administration online "Readiness Assessment," [2] and answered the way I would have back when I started my first venture:

"Do you have support from family and friends?"
No.
"Have you ever worked in a business similar to what you are starting?"
Not exactly.
"Have you ever taken a small business course or seminar?"
Nope.

I answered all the questions the best I could and hit the "submit" button. The assessment I received in return read:

"You're almost ready. Your answers indicate you possess many of the characteristics and skills necessary to be successful as an entrepreneur. Knowledge is power. Continue to plan and prepare yourself for starting a business."

Continue to plan? My original business approach could best be summed up by this description of an entrepreneur: "Someone

2. "Small Business Administration Assessment.
   eweb1.sba.gov/cams/training/business_primer/assessment.htm

who jumps off a cliff and builds their wings on the way down." Yep, that was me.

Let me take you back to my first cliff.

I held a few jobs over the years, including what many people used to think of as the ultimate good, secure job: I was a teacher. Then I got laid off. (So much for job security.) I also had various corporate sales jobs, expanding territory and increasing revenue for my bosses. And I hated every bit of it. I grew impatient as I waited for my good ideas to creep up the corporate ladder for approval. It was clear that I did not need to work for someone else.

Then I went to work for United Airlines in the 1980s. I still chafed at corporate ways, but United gave me the best job I ever had, and I was living the lifestyle I thought I wanted.

United was opening their international routes, and my job was to get travel agents and moneyed people on the plane and provide them with a luxurious experience. They would lodge at the best hotels and dine at the most acclaimed restaurants on those new routes. I would take 10 to 15 bigwigs at a time on trips to Japan, Hong Kong, and Hawaii to pitch the reasons that our service was better than TWA's or any other airline. I even took an underdeveloped territory and brought it up to $1 million. The clients loved me, and I loved traveling to all of these destinations, first class all the way. Ninety percent of the job was based on personality, and I certainly had the personality for that job.

Home base for my job was Rockefeller Center — 30 Rock — the heart of Manhattan. It was a wonderful, exciting world that was in every sense far, far away from my old jobs in places like Minnesota and Harrisburg, PA. I dressed in conservative chic, good wool and silk, and drove a bright red Fiat convertible. Top down, sunglasses on — that was me, the consummate single career girl. I had dates every other night. We'd party Thursday,

Friday, and Saturday, then take off on a flight on Sunday afternoon.

The trips I organized were filled with business savvy, self-made innovators, including women as well as men. I began to listen to the women in particular. I paid attention to their conversations, which shed light on a new world for me. These were women who worked for themselves and for their dreams. I soaked up the excitement of their ups and downs, their deals and failures and triumphs, the rejections they endured, and the recoveries they made.

I began to wonder: *Could I do that?*

The answer crystallized when I met Don King, the boxing promoter. He wanted to pitch an idea to United, and since he was headquartered in my territory, his call to United was routed to my office. So, off I went to meet him. His office was fantastic — in a beautiful brownstone building off Madison and 70th in Manhattan. The inside was gorgeous, with fine China and plush furnishings. It was simply stunning and impressive.

King himself was as wild as his office was beautiful. He was a taskmaster, ready to use his intimidating, 6'4" frame to ensure that things got done. And just as soon as he would lose his temper, he'd turn around and be a kind, welcoming, and funny host. He was chaotic with a big personality, but he never put on a front. And I liked that about him.

He was looking for a partnership with the airline which included "promotional consideration." This arrangement would mean that King would receive free or discounted United tickets for his fighters and their entourage. In exchange, United would get advertising in the form of messaging ("Promotional consideration given by United Airlines") at the end of the televised fights. United would also get extra paid business from those who were flying with King's entourage to the fights in Las Vegas or Los Angeles.

I pitched the idea to United, and they turned down my proposal four times. Maybe they didn't think Don King's spiked hair and loud mouth fit United's corporate image. Maybe they thought he was too outrageous for them to give him the "promotional consideration" which was so coveted at the time. But I kept trying, and I did my research. I created a spreadsheet which showed United how many of the same men who read the "Wall Street Journal" first thing in the morning (their target audience) would then flip to the tabloid sports pages or pick up "The Daily News" to follow the fights and basketball games later in the day. Once I showed them that their audience overlapped with Don King's, United finally made the deal, which opened up $300,000 to $500,000 in new revenue for the company.

The success I created for United amplified my internal conversation about striking out on my own. Why couldn't I go into business and do for myself what I had been doing for United?

Not long after, I drove to a quick print shop, arranged for some business cards and some stationery, and opened MAPP Productions. I went into the public relations/publicity business in my hometown of Newark, New Jersey.

One day, two guys I knew came to MAPP Productions and asked me to serve as a consultant to help them start their construction business. At first, they just wanted me to set up the company for them. Then they offered me a partnership. Their plan was to go after the minority-designated contracts that public projects were required to offer. That affirmative action policy was designed to increase minority participation in public construction. That's how MZM Construction was born.

I didn't know anything about construction. I had not taken any business courses. I didn't know about writing a business plan or how to estimate a job. I would not have had the right answers for any should-you-go-into-*this*-business-for-yourself tests. And because I learned on the go, I made mistakes on my journey. I'll tell you about those later on, but for now, let me just say that I don't recommend the "jump off the cliff" approach.

To know yourself is the key: Are you really a leader? Or are you really meant to be a manager or employee? There is no shame in being a manager or an employee. However, there may be a treacherous path ahead for those who are more comfortable being employees who then jump into trying to lead their own businesses.

Are you willing to risk your own money and live with the prospect that your employees and vendors must get paid even when you do not? Do you have the unwavering persistence that running your own business will take?

Of all the self-assessment quizzes I've come across, the one I really liked was featured in *Crain's Chicago Business* in September, 2013: "Do you really have the mind of an entrepreneur?"[3] That quiz asked ten questions and provided "hints" that were really sound counsel as to how you should think if you are trying to make a decision about going out on your own.

By the way, as I write this, the U.S. is just beginning to recover from a horrendous economic slump. People have lost their jobs as many fulltime employees have been replaced by part-timers who won't get benefits, raises, or pensions. Simultaneously, consultants and independent contractors have created new businesses out of what they used to do for their bosses.

Trying times often present opportunity for those willing to try something new. Can you afford not to take the risk?

3. "Do you have the mind of an entrepreneur," Crain's Chicago Business Online. http://www.chicagobusiness.com/article/20130928/ISSUE02/130829939/do-you-have-the-mind-of-an-entrepreneur

Chapter 4

Manage Your Ego, Control Your Fear

Let's call your ego that part of you that looks at the accomplishments of others, or at any business success story and says: *"I can do that. Maybe not on the same scale. Maybe not right away. Bu, there is no reason I can't do what those others are doing."*

Now, let's call your fear the part of you that, even in the face of 101 things that support your dream and urge you to push forward, make you say, *"Not now,"* or, *"I'd better not."*

If you didn't have some level of confidence in the first place, you wouldn't even be thinking about starting your own business or enterprise. You would probably have an idea that hard work, as well as some pitfalls and risks, lie ahead. But the potential challenges are not going to stop you from jumping off the metaphorical cliff and starting your own business. Without some opposing force, that confidence will swell and create a significant ego.

It's your fear — a healthy dose of appropriate fear — that will make you assess the risks, get advice, come up with a plan, and then double check everything. In other words, I am advising you to build some wings before you jump!

But, of course, too much fear will keep you from taking even calculated risks. If you are totally beholden to your fear, you'll never grow. You'll listen to the thoughts and opinions of others more than yourself because you'll think they're more reliable. Then, you'll never know what *you* are actually capable of.

So, you need to learn to manage your ego and control your fear so that they don't manage and control you. Instead of operating from ego or fear, I now operate from strength and confidence. When I falter, I don't let my ego tell me, "They took advantage of me," or, "It wasn't my fault." Instead, my strength tells me that I can grow and learn from those mistakes. It helps me get through. And fear doesn't keep me from taking risks or trying new things. My confidence shows me that I can do it, and if it doesn't work out how I want it to, I'll find a solution.

If you are thinking about starting a business, one of your earliest steps should be to assess your strengths. I went into business for myself because something inside of me reminded me that I had a talent for dealing with people. I could figure out how to get things done, and I had a track record of having taken on countless new projects and succeeding. The entire time, I had been making my bosses and supervisors look really, really good. So, why couldn't I do all of those things in my own business for myself? Why couldn't I be the boss and reap the rewards of all of my efforts?

I had never taken a business course, but my corporate life had given me a lot of diverse work experience, which had helped me to develop a number of skills. For example, since I had worked in sales for major corporations, I had to be an independent actor, a self-starter. I also had to work with numbers and file financial reports. Additionally, it was my responsibility to figure out strategies to find new customers and expand sales. Since I had successfully staged promotional events as another part of my job responsibilities, my first entrepreneurial idea was to create a public relations firm of my own. At the time, this seemed like a solid idea.

Even though my experience working for others gave me some useful tools, it was clear that I simply did not fit the corporate mold. I didn't always get along with the higher ups or my colleagues. I was impatient as I waited for those who I worked with to recognize the value of my ideas, which inevitably proved themselves once they made it through the numbingly slow process of review and approval by others.

So, it's fair to say that my motivation to become an entrepreneur and leave a "traditional" job behind was somewhat rooted in fear, but even more so in my strength. In the back of my mind, I felt worried that sooner or later the rebel in me would get me fired. The rebel in me did not know how to be quiet or not fight for opportunities if what I thought I deserved was being awarded to others. I was headstrong, and in the 1980s, that kind of fight could get you immediately pushed out the door of corporate America. And when I thought, *"Might as well go out on my own steam, with my own plan,"* I had the strength to actually follow through.

Is leaving a "good job" part of your fear? If so, consider this: layoffs are common now in industries that rarely let employees go in the past. That means your "good job" today could be gone tomorrow. Your "good job" today does not offer the security it used to.

If you want to create your own business, you must find the strength and confidence to work around any reasonable fears. For example, perhaps you can work part-time while you build your dream. Working part-time will keep your income flowing into your bank account, while you begin to create the foundation for your business. In my case, working part-time when I was creating my business was a very wise choice: I had a degree in physical education, and I had worked for a short time in the past as a gym teacher. My credentials allowed me to work as a trainer in a gym while I built my public relations firm. Opportunities then opened up for me to do promotional work for the gym and even some public relations for the local YMCA. I also drove for a limousine company, which very fortuitously put me in direct contact with people who could use my public relations services and well afford them. It appeared to be the perfect setup for attracting new clients to my brand new business.

Then my big break came when Donald Payne was elected as New Jersey's first African American Congressman in 1988. I had been doing some public relations work for one of the Newark councilmen, and when Payne's people put out a call for someone to set up his inaugural event, my name was mentioned. Payne's people called and told me about the expectations they held for the planning and publicity for this huge and very public event. I confidently replied, "I can do that!" — and I did.

I decided to focus the event on an historical angle. I booked the Charles Sumner School in Washington, D.C. for Payne's daytime inaugural event. (The Sumner School, which is now a museum, was among the very first schools for African American students in the District of Columbia. In 1877 the Sumner School held the first-ever high school graduation for Black students.) I also booked the Rayburn House Office Building for Payne's evening events. Then I found the caterers and handled every moving part to put the whole thing together, even though I didn't know a soul in Washington D.C.!

Because of the success of that one event, my reputation for staging successful, big occasions began to blossom. I was delighted. I knew I had found my passion. My creative mind was super-charged because I knew I could get things done, and I could figure everything else out on the way.

Soon I had about four or five clients. But that is not enough to sustain oneself in a business. It was not a big pot. I found myself hustling to bring in more people. I was busy, but I was not making a lot of money. In fact, I was not even close to making my dreams of wealth come true. Still, I had to acknowledge that I was happier than I'd ever been before.

The business eked by on referrals, and then, one day, one of the referrals led to the two friends who wanted my help in starting their construction business. After I shared all of the ways I could contribute to their company, they soon brought me in as a partner. That was the start of what is now my company, MZM.

My confidence said, *"Jump,"* and I took the leap. Simultaneously, my more cautious, but still strong, side said, *"Learn."* And I did that, too.

Fortunately for us, from small municipal projects to big federal ones, Affirmative Action mandates created the legal obligation for publicly financed construction projects to include the participation of minority and women-owned firms. On average, 25 percent of any contract had to include the participation of minority firms, and there needed to be 17 percent participation by women-owned firms.

In the early days of Affirmative Action, some scandals evolved called, "set asides," in which a so-called minority firm, would be awarded a contract. In reality, the minority firm was basically a shell operation to help a big, white, male contractor show minority participation on paper. Nowadays, a company must be certified by the state or federal government to attest to true minority ownership. Prior to these changes, however, some minority firms would get a set aside contract for $150,000 as subcontractors to the big firms, who would actually be handling most of the job. The minority firms were not set up to do the work, nor were they interested in doing the work. They would be content to take $15,000 for the use of their names, and let the big contractor do the work and keep the rest of the money.

That wasn't my idea of how my enterprise should run. I didn't know how to read a contract, nor did I know how to read a blueprint, but I knew how to learn. So, my company could do what it was contracted to do and earn all the money it was supposed to get!

In 1992, the same year MZM was born, we received a small contract related to the construction of the New Jersey Performing Arts Center (NJPAC.) The venue was to be built in downtown Newark with public support and private philanthropy. NJPAC needed a minority company to meet the diversity requirement. Starting with a $50,000 landscaping contract, MZM ultimately landed $4 million in business involving NJPAC over the following four years. (In addition, we also put in the sewer sanitation lines. So, if you go there and flush a toilet, think of me!)

"Whenever I don't know something, I go educate myself."

Understand this: I was out in the middle of this huge, visible project, and I was dumber than dumb. Whenever I feel like I don't know something, I go someplace to educate myself. So, I went to "landscaping school." By that, I mean I approached some of the big contractors for information. They told me all about landscaping, excavation, and planting greenery. I *had* to learn. In my mind, anything less would be crazy. I couldn't just sign a piece of paper and say I was on a job I didn't understand.

I also heard the late Gus Henningburg, the founder and president of the not-for-profit, Greater Newark Urban Coalition, in my ear. Gus spent much of his life fighting to integrate the construction trades and make African Americans true economic beneficiaries of public construction and development projects. He once told me, "Do not be a pass-through. Learn everything there is to learn out there. This window will pass. When it does, you have to be prepared."

I also kept hearing the voices of those wealthy, successful people I'd met on my flights when I worked for United. *"Know your game,"* they always preached to me. *"Understand what you're doing."*

I used my contractor mentors as sounding boards and relied on them to provide insight whenever I did anything.

In the midst of all this, my two partners asked me to buy them out. This was not really a big deal financially, since we had each contributed only $2,500 to start up. I gave them back the money they had initially put in.

Then the accolades started coming in. A Black woman in construction on the job at NJPAC made a perfect feature for a news story. I appeared on television and there were articles written about me and my company in the newspapers. Very quickly, MZM's name was spreading throughout the community. MZM was a big deal, which made *me* a big deal in the eyes of those who could see what I did, but who had no idea that I was learning as I was going and making it look really good as I went.

I fed off of that notoriety. I looked at what I had accomplished and decided I could step away from my mentors and go out entirely on my own. But I stepped away too soon, and my ego led the way...

Chapter 5

Are You Prepared to Go Broke?

You're looking for advice about starting your own business, so the last thing you want to hear about is the possibility of going broke, right?

Well, if you are thinking about creating a business you need to spend some time examining your beliefs and thoughts about money. Getting it, spending it, and losing it — losing your shirt, in fact.

"If the idea is just to make money, you've already failed before you begin."

Let me start by telling you what I think about money and building a business: Successful entrepreneurs tend to be those who are willing to live in a car if that's what it takes to keep going. They are not going to be deterred from their dream, and their dream is not just about making money. I will say this yet again: If the idea is just to make money, you've already failed before you begin. Money is the measure of how successful your dream is. You've got to be clear about that point, and you've also got to absolutely love what you do. The money will come and go.

According to the U.S. Small Business Administration, about half of all new business establishments survive five years or more and about one-third survive 10 years or more. Between March of 2021 and March of 2022, the SBA said 1.2 million new small business establishment were born, and just under 843,000 closed their doors.[4]

One study by Bruce D. Phillips of the National Federation of Independent Business, and the late Bruce A. Kirchhoff, who was director of the technological entrepreneurship program at New Jersey Institute of Technology, reported that only 39.8 percent of businesses with 500 employees or fewer were still going after six years on average. According to that study, there were a wide range of differences when it came to the survival rates depending on the type of enterprise.[5]

However, they found nothing as bleak as the claims by the then Republican Kentucky Senator and perennial presidential candidate, Rand Paul, who proclaimed that nine out of ten new businesses don't make it past their toddler years. As a "Washington Post" article on the subject pointed out, there is no

---

4. "Small Business Administration Office of Advocacy 2023 Small Business Economic Profile."

https://advocacy.sba.gov/wp-content/uploads/2023/11/2023-Small-Business-Economic-Profile-US.pdf

5. "Formation, Growth and Survival; Small Firm Dynamics in the U.S. Economy" (1989)

Bruce D. Phillips of the National Federation of Independent Business and Bruce A. Kirchhoff, director of the technological entrepreneurship program at New Jersey Institute of Technology.

University of Illinois at Urbana-Champaign's Academy for Entrepreneurial Leadership Historical Research Reference in Entrepreneurship.

good data as to how many of the businesses that appear to "die" actually live on in mergers or acquisitions that formed bigger, and perhaps better, new enterprises.[6]

The numbers may not be as dire as Rand Paul suggested, but you must accept the fact that failure is a possibility. There may be companies that have not gone through a serious reversal, but I will bet that those companies are few and far between. I took my company, MZM, to the brink of bankruptcy in the early years. However, 15 years later, I'm still here.

So, how do *you* feel about money?

As I said before, some people have a paycheck mentality, the kind of personality that does not want to worry about the possibility of failure or having to work on a recovery. The idea of collecting income via anything other than a steady, consistent manner scares most people.

"If your business isn't growing, it is dying."

Some people try to run their business with that same paycheck mentality. They want to hang onto the same clients and dip into the same pot of revenue from their original client base. They never look to the right or left for new clients or new opportunities, nor do they look to the future to expand their businesses in new and meaningful ways. Even if their businesses do not go under, they are not going to grow. They avoid change without realizing change is necessary to get to the next level. Making changes should be done with care. Remember, running a business and not

---

6. "Do nine out of 10 new businesses fail, as Rand Paul claims?" Washington Post, January 27, 2014.
www.washingtonpost.com/blogs/fact-checker/wp/2014/01/27/do-9-out-of-10-new-businesses-fail-as-rand-paul-claims/

growing and changing with it will allow stagnation to set in, which can be fatal to an organization. In any industry, you can expect some customer attrition each year, so if your business isn't growing, it is dying.

Other entrepreneurs think their businesses are all about spending money on themselves. They expect that two days after they start, their businesses should pay off with their dream house, the car they always wanted, and all of the necessities for the lifestyle to which they want to become accustomed. Taking money out of their businesses comes before putting money back into the businesses they create. They may be the ones Rand Paul was talking about when he came up with his nine out of ten "losers" statistic. Very few startups can turn enough profit to support a "Me-First" boss.

It is also a mistake to spend more than you can afford on your business. Construction is an industry run heavily on equipment. Initially, I leased instead of buying what I needed so my expenditures were appropriate to what I was bringing in. I kept everything lean.

On the other hand, I know two bright guys who partnered in a tech startup. They had a good idea and the experience to make it happen. Coming from a corporate background, they thought their new company needed to have every single department their corporate employer had. So, they invested heavily in human resources and some related support services — and promptly went under before their first anniversary.

My disaster came in a different way when my ego went marching ahead of my fear. This is how it happened...

As I mentioned, my company was featured on television and in the news. A committee working on the expansion of a church in Newark saw the publicity about me and my company and reached out to me. They wanted me to do the excavation for the church project and lay the concrete.

I initially turned them down because my instincts told me I wasn't ready. I knew how to move dirt, but I did not know a thing about concrete. This was an opportunity, but it just seemed too big. I didn't even have a clue about costing out the job. They said that this wasn't a problem, as they would provide the right people to help, including estimators.

I was a naive little girl, sitting in a roomful of people who were admired and respected in the community. They promised they were going to help me. And remember, I was using the "extreme business" method, in which I was growing my wings on the way down. So, I jumped off the cliff.

They hooked me up with an estimator — their guy — who told me the amount I was supposed to charge for my work. All I asked was, "Are you sure?"

He replied, "Yes."

Here's a quick lesson for you: *YOU must be in full control of the decisions that matter when it comes to what you charge and what you spend.* Leaving those decisions to anyone other than yourself, or someone you have hired, vetted, and trust is insane. Even if you have full faith and trust in someone else who you've assigned to render an analysis of your income and expenditures, you must have enough knowledge to know if the numbers make sense. I didn't have the knowledge or a vetted analyst, and it cost me.

The men in charge of the church expansion must have known I was way under on the numbers. The job should have cost $4.25 per square foot and the estimator — their estimator — told me to do it for $1.70 per square foot. So, I did the work. But they kept stringing me along instead of paying me. My payroll was $25,000 a week, so I kept borrowing money. I might have gotten away with it if I'd used nonunion workers, but in the 1990s, everything in Newark was hardcore union, and the contract required union labor.

I kept borrowing. I kept going and going.

Then my clients had me sign a document, a "waiver of lien" that said "all material men" had been paid. I signed it and had it notarized, because the church guys told me I wouldn't get paid if I didn't. However, because it was a notarized lie — I had not paid everybody — they could then refuse to pay me. I went to court and tried to fight it, but I never got my money.

I signed the waiver of lien because I thought I had to. I had no lawyer. You read that right: I had no lawyer advising me. I had no team, nobody to tell me what not to do, no one on my side to protect me. I let their guy estimate my project. I trusted them.

Okay, I was an idiot. I trusted them and they were not even my friends. I was operating out of ego and fear — I didn't want them to think badly of me. Back then, I would trust anybody who seemed to be doing better in life than I was. The result was that I get screwed.

I lost $1 million — the money I had borrowed to do the work. Then I made 100 more mistakes while I was trying to self-correct and make more money to pay back everything I'd borrowed. I decided not to declare bankruptcy in part because I had secured a Small Business Administration guaranteed loan from a bank. Under the terms of the SBA loan, bankruptcy or not, the bank could take everything I had. But the real deal was this: I had promised to pay back the loan, every penny, and in my mind that meant I couldn't walk away.

How did I get through it? I have a gift for survival that I just can't explain. From 1999 to 2007, I hardly made any profit, but whatever I brought in went to paying off my debts.

I remembered the things my father told me: *Pay your bills. Finish what you start. Be responsible.*

That financial disaster taught me a lot, but experience can be too harsh a teacher. Sometimes, extreme business just doesn't work. Jumping off the cliff without having all my ducks in a row almost sank me. I want you to avoid traps like this one, which almost killed my business. This lesson was not just about failure for me. It was about how I recovered. So here is some advice:

Know your game. That was advice that I had been given by one of my contractor mentors, and I should have followed it. There was so much I didn't know about pricing the work. After my fall from financial grace, and during my recovery, I took classes. I learned to read blueprints and estimates and I got my Masters in Business Administration. But before that, I let ignorance run my machine. I was ignorant when it came to reading the numbers that would have clearly demonstrated my profit or loss. I let someone else, my customer, set the numbers. I was ignorant because I kept working, thinking that sooner or later they would pay me.

Know your customers before you get into bed with them. Your customer is not your business partner and not necessarily your friend. You have every right to interview the customer. In truth, you must. You can't just be excited about the project.

Accept the fact that you are going to make mistakes. Failure comes as part of the package. You could lose your shirt even if you don't make a mistake. You can do everything right and get smacked down because of a market slump that thins out your customers or their orders. You could hit the skids because of a change in technology that makes what you do obsolete. Perhaps a bigger, more aggressive competitor will skim away your customers.

As an entrepreneur, you cannot be afraid of failure or of losing money until things stabilize. But you must do all you can to minimize the number of mistakes and the effect of your fumbles and stumbles. When a failure occurs, look for the lesson and figure out what you learned that will prevent such a thing from happening again.

Most of all, forgive yourself. After my debacle, I spent a lot of time in victim mode. I blamed myself. I was depressed. I ate poorly because I was stressed and lived on a fast-food budget. I gained weight. It was a dark time, and that time lasted for several years. Now, if I lose a contract or if something goes wrong, my focus is not on being a victim, but on mitigating the mistake as quickly as possible and avoiding anything that comes close to a repetition of that error.

It's not about blame; it's about business.

Chapter 6

Building Your Team: Part I

Perhaps you're thinking: *"My team is just me and the boxes of product in my basement,"* or, *"My team is however many relatives I can bribe to lend me a hand when I need it."*

According to the U.S. Census Bureau, the vast majority of U.S. businesses — 75 percent of them — have no payroll and no permanent employees.[7] Most of those enterprises are self-employed people, who are running unincorporated businesses. Their "businesses" may not even be their primary source of income. These businesses account for 75 percent of all U.S firms, but only for 3.4 percent of all business receipts. They are small and most of them are going to stay that way.

If you are happy and content with where going it alone has gotten you, congratulations, keep it up. But if you want to grow, you will need a team to work with and grow with you. That does not mean you have to stick a lot of people on your payroll. You can hire freelancers as needed to handle a particular problem or

---

7. "Statistics about Business Size (including Small Business)" from the U.S. Census Bureau (Statistics of U.S. Businesses, 2007.

www.census.gov/econ/smallbus.html

to work on a particular project. They do the job, you pay them, and then they go on their merry way. You can always bring them back when and if you need them.

If, on the other hand, you need part-time or full-time employees, because you've got consistent things to do, you need certain people to do them, and you have the revenues to support the operating expense, hiring employees is what you do. There is no right or wrong answer; it is a matter of what you need and what you can afford.

Also, don't think of your team as just the people who are required to sell, produce, or pack up your product. Whatever the size of your operation, you should have a retinue of professionals and advisors on your team, and it is best to have them in place before you need them.

This is a scenario that is often used to help small business owners understand why they need a certain set of professionals on their side: You get the call from The Big Widget Company offering a contract that will get the boxes out of your basement and push your fledgling business forward. Big Widget is sending over the contract for your attorney to review and requests a copy of your certificate of insurance. You realize you are going to need some cash to gear up for handling the deal. If you hang up, thinking, *"Who? What, and huh?"* you lack the key elements of the team that any business should have: An attorney, an accountant, a bookkeeper, an insurance agent, and a banker to consult with as needed.

When working with these professionals, it's important to pay them accordingly. It will be useful to do a cost/benefit analysis for their services to show the true value of having these ancillary team members by your side: Discuss what they charge ahead of time, then evaluate what you're getting for that fee. This includes peace of mind; consider what you're risking *without* enlisting their help. Ask around to find out which professionals and firms other small business owners use. Interview the people or firms you think you want for your team to see if they can meet your specific needs. How much do they know about businesses of your kind and size?

I didn't have that kind of team in place when I made my $1 million mistake. I had a knack for booking business, for networking, and for going out to get contracts and customers. I did not have a natural background for operating a business. I would fall, then get up and keep running. I was learning the hard way. That's because I also lacked another team, the kind I strongly urge you to build for yourself: An advisory board.

An advisory board is not a board of directors. It is typically not paid, has no legal authority over your company, and cannot kick you out or take over. An advisory board consists of a group of individuals who come together regularly to help you work on your business in general or on a specific goal.

Why do you need an advisory board? You can't go it alone; you need the feedback, the extra minds to say, *"But what about x? And how about y?"* You need people to share their experiences with you. I formed my advisory board as I was climbing out of the hole. If I had formed one earlier, I might have avoided that hole altogether. For years, we met once a month. I would bring my advisors my company's details for the month, and they would give me their feedback.

Invite people you admire, people whose opinions and judgment you can trust. You might include one person who is in the same industry as you and others who are not, but who are great at what they do. Their job is to give you their objective viewpoints.

There are some formalized groups which serve the same function, but you often need to hit a certain level of revenue to join them. This may interest you later in your journey, but they're not necessary to help you get started.

On my advisory board sat the ex-president of a major East Coast grocery chain, a partner from a large accounting firm, an attorney from one of the top law firms in the state, and another attorney who specialized in construction firms. To this day, they are still with me and I can email them and get their input quickly. There are also times when I will bring them in for a sit-down session.

"Why would such people want to help me? Why would the ex-president of anything take time out for me?" you ask. Thinking that way is thinking from an "I'm broke" mentality. Ask, and the worst that can happen is that they say, "No." Part of your job is to network, to go out into the world to sell the idea of you and your business. You need to meet people and talk to them. When anyone hands you a business card and says, *"Feel free to call me,"* take the offer seriously and call them. They may be the perfect advisor for you.

If you just started your enterprise yesterday, you may not get much interest. But if you have been around for a few years, and you are building your company and your reputation, you might be surprised as to who might be interested in helping you. People who have made it in business often have a sincere desire to reach back and help someone else make it. I do not know anyone who is successful in business who did not get a hand up along the way. Almost all successful people have had mentors. That's why most of them are more than happy to mentor someone else.

Again, advisory boards are usually not paid, but I always arranged our meetings over dinner and paid for my advisors' meals out of respect for their time and travel. If you do the same, you'll find that the relationships you build are worth the investment.

At the very least you need a trusted lieutenant. I had that in the two partners who initially formed my construction company with me. Not until I bought them out did I realize how valuable their input had been. They were the yin to my yang. We would go back and forth in conversation all the time. You are never going to see all the things coming at you, or examine every angle, while you are trying to move your business forward.

When I started to grow my business, I had to admit that I did not have the financial acumen to manage operations at the next level. I would hire people who I knew were not necessarily the best fit because I was worried about the budget. That is a really good way to set yourself up for failure and lose a significant amount of money. It was my partners who helped me to see that it's better to invest in people who will actually help your business thrive. It's worth waiting until you can financially justify making that investment as opposed to jumping the gun and hiring someone who is less qualified. They were also the ones who motivated me to go back to school and work on my MBA.

Your business partners, a family member who is good at business, someone who does not let you make too many emotional moves, or a person who helps you make more objective moves could be your trusted lieutenant.

Now, I have two attorneys who fill that role, and I don't make a major move without them.

Chapter 7

Building Your Team: Part II

One of the best things about owning a business is that you can put people to work. However, I have an Achilles heel, a weak spot that has been one of my greatest failures. I've tended to be too quick to hire and too slow to fire.

Here's an example: I hired an executive assistant. She was a nice young woman, and she probably would have made a really good receptionist or clerk, if that was what I'd needed. But this was a much more dynamic job with a higher salary attached, and the young lady couldn't think past go or pay attention to detail. On top of that, she didn't have the experience or skills she claimed she had on her resume.

I had given her a job description that spelled out her duties, one of which was going through the mail and organizing documents. One day, I found a pile of mail that she hadn't opened and a pile of papers she'd never filed, which meant that important documents were unorganized or completely neglected. When I asked her to draft a letter, she would say she didn't know what to put in it. When she was supposed to manage my calendar, she said she had never done that task before.

Despite all of this clearly being in her job description, I ended up loading the stamp machine myself and went through a stack of papers she'd stuffed under her desk. I was doing her work while also paying her a substantial salary.

Then there was the day it snowed just before the Super Bowl, when MZM had the snow removal contract at MetLife Stadium. We were under a magnifying glass, and there were lots of eyes watching us and TV cameras on us to see if we could really clear the snow in a timely fashion. Even though she was in New York City, a short ride away from our New Jersey office, she didn't show up at work. I was in California, but the rest of the MZM team was humming along in East Rutherford. Buses were on their way to pick up the crew and the guys were arriving at the office, but my office wasn't open because my executive assistant hadn't shown up. I had to call someone from a neighboring office to open MZM's doors so the crew could get the job done.

She never knew what to do, but she never asked any questions either. You have to ask in order to learn. She sat there all day long, while I needed a self-starter. She was reactionary when I needed someone who anticipated my needs. She didn't understand that a handwritten note was personal mail and shouldn't be opened, but a business envelope with a label on it was business mail that she should go through.

She had to go, but I don't like to fire people. I don't want to be a negative source in their hearts, and I know people need to keep their jobs. But I needed a person who could do the things I needed them to do.

My executive assistant wasn't assisting me. Yet, it took everything I had to get up the courage to let her go. I kept waiting and putting off what I knew I should do. That's my pattern: When someone needs to be fired, I keep hoping it will get better, but it never does.

I finally fired her, and I was absolutely miserable. I felt the guilt even though it was the correct move for my business.

Soon after, I went away for a weekend business retreat with my executive coach. It costs me a fortune to have a coach, but it is well worth it. She helped me realize that when prospective employees come in the door and say they can perform a task, I want to believe them. But for all I know, they could have cut and pasted something off the internet and plopped it right on their resume. I wasn't doing my due diligence to make sure they had what it took to fit into my organization.

"The best way to avoid firing people is to hire more strategically."

I learned that the best way to avoid firing people is to hire more strategically. At the time, I was okay with hiring my friends or people who I liked without really looking at their level of expertise. It was more comfortable for me to bring on people I knew, as I wasn't yet confident enough to believe that I deserved to hire the best talent on the market. This was a mistake. Even if you can hire people you know at a slightly lower rate, it is so much more important to make the investment in a top-notch individual. As previously discussed, this is a much stronger strategic decision for your business in the long run.

It was also important for me to admit that I am not an HR professional. Instead of trying to do that job myself, I decided to bring on a fractional HR specialist to dive into the pool of applicants, analyze resumes, and find people with the right skills and deliverables. When you're scaling a small business, you need people who are multi-taskers with a wide skillset. You need people who are adaptable. The right HR professional is capable of finding those people for you and will therefore help your business to grow with fewer bumps in the road.

According to a 2012 article on Entrepreneur.com, every small business needs five types of employees: one who will share knowledge and skills by teaching others, one who always wants to learn new things and stay current, someone who can adapt and solve any problem, someone who boosts morale through positivity, and someone who is going to find ways to innovate and challenge the status quo. [8]

Whether you hire those five, just one, or fifty depends, of course, on what you need. No one formula is going to fit every business. Not having enough people on board can be as expensive as having too many on the payroll. I have some full-time employees, but I also hire project managers just to see a specific assignment through. If they do a good job, they may be brought back for additional work.

I met a man whose brother has been working for him for years as the operations officer. His brother simply cannot get the job done, and therefore there has been no growth in that business for years. The owner wants to know what to do about his brother. Why have the brother's faults suddenly become intolerable after all these years? Could it be that certain issues are more easily overlooked in good times than during a challenging economy?

In any case, the business owner often knows what needs to happen, but when it comes to a family member, firing that person is especially hard. Your business is not supposed to be a parking lot for incompetent relatives. That doesn't mean you shouldn't hire competent, qualified relatives. But, along with the usual employee problems, you have to be prepared for the collateral damage when the relative/employee fails, or when there is a

---

8. "The 5 Employees Every Small Business Needs," Entreprenuer.com February, 2013. www.entrepreneur.com/article/225643

downturn and you have to let your kin go. The family will be angry. Can you handle the emotional dumping that is guaranteed to come as a result?

Also, be careful about being such a good friend that you stop being a good employer.

As I said, when I first started MZM, I made my staff my friends. I shared my stories and mingled. I wanted to be liked, so I only hired people that I liked. Then when it came time to get some work done, I yelled, and they were puzzled.

"What's the problem?" they'd ask. "You've been letting us get away with it until now."

Except for Montana, every state allows employers to have an at-will employment policy. That means absent any prior agreement or contract between them, the employer may terminate any employee at any time, for any reason, or for no reason at all. You cannot, however, fire someone because of race, age, gender, religion, national origin, sexual orientation, or disability. It is also illegal to fire someone who complains about health or safety violations, discrimination or harassment, or illegal activity in the workplace.[9]

Try to intervene and address performance issues before they require termination. If there is an issue and firing is potentially on the horizon, be sure to document that person's performance issues before you let that employee go. Keep a record of poor performance, tardiness, employee evaluations, and disciplinary actions. Discuss these problems directly with the employee and put together a performance improvement plan (often called a PIP) to get them on the right track.

---

9. "How to Fire an Employee and Stay within the Law" SBA Blogs, April 30, 2012. http://www.sba.gov/blogs/how-fire-employee-and-stay-within-law

If that still doesn't work, it's probably time to part ways. Bring documented performance problems to refer to when you sit down with someone for the termination conversation and maintain those records even after the employee is gone. The documentation may become necessary if the employee decides to sue or to claim harassment—whether or not they have a valid claim.

Chapter 8

Leadership

When I started out, I was a multi-tasker. If something needed to be done, or if something went wrong, it was "Marge to the rescue." If the copy machine needed fixing, I would go tinker with it. If something went wrong in accounting, I would do accounting. If something went wrong in the field, I went out into the field. That made me a great manager, but a terrible leader!

A leader needs to be great at delegating because they are usually too busy attending to the big picture to handle all the little details personally. Of course, like everything else I'm telling you, this advice must be adjusted to the kind of operation you are running. If your business consists of just you and the boxes in the basement, you have to do everything. There is no one to whom you can delegate. (But I have two questions: First, are you leading yourself in the right direction to get the boxes out of the basement? And second, if you're struggling just to keep up, *should* there be someone else to whom you can delegate?)

If you are working full-paced, 16 hours-a-day, seven days a week to get everything done, do you have a business? Or do you have a very demanding job? As I've said before, if you're content with the way things are, fine. But if you're busy spending every minute working *in* the business, you will not have time to work *on* the business, to make it grow, to build wealth, to create a legacy. Those are the things that a leader does.

If you are in a position to delegate but aren't doing so, is it because you don't trust others? Are you fearful about bringing in someone who might steal your concept? Didn't you get that lawyer to help you protect your intellectual property, as well as your business property? Do you worry about turning even part of the work over to others because they might mess everything up?

They probably won't as long as you've picked the right staff and advisors, you've mapped out the direction in which your business should go, and you're clear about the supplies and the resources you need to get there.

So, what makes a good leader? In my case, the answer was time. I had to grow into a position of leadership, and I am still evolving. I think, however, that natural leadership qualities can often be detected at an early age.

Your environment, as well as the people you surround yourself with, can certainly influence your skills or your ability to be a good leader. Just look at Oprah Winfrey. We've all heard about how hard Oprah's early years were. The child of unmarried teenage parents, she lived with her mother, was abused by male relatives, and seemed destined for a troubled life. Then her father had her come live with him and her entire life changed. He was a barber who ran his own business, giving Oprah a new kind of role model to emulate. Oprah was encouraged to get an education and stretch her wings. What if she had never moved in with her father? Would she ever have become the billionaire media mogul she is today?

Good leaders have confidence and are not afraid to make a decision. If you make a mistake, you get back up. Over time, the good leaders will make better and wiser decisions because they will get up and learn. Then they will position themselves to do better, so that over time, they will be better. They will make wise decisions, which is high on my list of the qualities a leader must have.

I learned how to make those wise decisions through failure. My journey included a lot of trying, learning, and adapting. To put it simply, I did not know what I did not know. I certainly found out, though, and found the right path along the way.

One of the key things I learned through this process was that I was working too much *in* the business and not enough *on* the business. I was too bogged down by the little details that I was better off trusting others to handle, and that I needed to learn to direct and delegate. Trust your team and assemble the staff the business requires. Leaders are not just looking for "yes" men; they look for the right mix of people.

Leaders do their homework. They seek out information, they question, they research, and they don't just focus on their own business niche. That's why leaders seek to learn from the best, and why their early years can help to shape them.

In my case, my independent spirit was not nurtured at home, but was fed elsewhere. My parents called me "rambunctious" and "uncontrollable," while my teachers called me "precocious." Being active in church and community groups helped to prepare me to eventually become a leader. Being a part of these communities helped me to remain grounded and gave me a solid base of support that I found very helpful through the difficult times.

One particular experience I had as part of the Baptist Student Union was extremely formative. At the age of 16, I was selected to speak at HBCU college campuses all over the country on behalf of my youth group. I was always articulate, and this trip helped me to forge that skillset and turned me into the professional speaker I am today. Through those engagements, I saw that people look to leaders for truth and guidance.

"I made more mistakes along the way, but I never made the same mistake twice."

When everything failed, I knew that nothing would do except for me to work my way out. So, I shifted into overdrive to pay my debts. I made more mistakes along the way, but I never made the same mistake twice. That's when I started my advisory board to help minimize the chances of new disasters. I went back to school and stopped telling myself I could wing it. Figuring things out on the fly was no longer an option when it came to my business. As I worked out of that deep, dark hole, I became the leader who built MZM into what it is today — a multi-million-dollar company.

My decision making became more powerful as my learning curve improved. I let go of the pride that insisted I could figure things out by myself. I operated with humility and ensured that I was adapting as much as necessary.

Through it all, I always maintained my integrity. Even though there was an option to file bankruptcy, I wanted to keep my work and pay those whom I had promised to pay. I did just that and took on a tremendous amount of debt, but all of my people were taken care of. No one else was out a dime they were owed because it was important for me to follow through. I had signed my name saying they would be paid for their work, and so they were.

I hold to that code to this day. Hold to your word, as keeping your integrity intact is a significant contributor to your reputation and success. It keeps you grounded, ensures that everyone always has a positive experience working with you, and reminds you that you are only as good as your last project.

To summarize:

- Leaders seek to learn what they don't know.
- Leaders work with humility.
- Leaders adapt.
- Leaders thrive under pressure.
- Leaders always act with integrity.

If you can be these things, you are already well on your way.

Chapter 9

Listen

I love the TV show *Shark Tank*. Entrepreneurs who think they've come up with the "next big thing" try to get a panel of well-known businesspeople — the Sharks — to invest in a newborn organization.

Time after time I hear the Sharks tell those pitching to them, "You're not listening to us." Invariably, the Sharks criticize the way the project is being marketed, or they point out how the person's competitors are selling something as good, or better, for less. The entrepreneurs should understand the value of any advice they get from big money investors like Mark Cuban, Barbara Corcoran, Daymond John, or Kevin O'Leary. But instead of bowing to wisdom, the wanna-be-moguls keep babbling about how they believe in what they are doing. They don't want to change, so they don't hear the truth in the advice they are getting. Denial makes them deaf. And, of course, at some point the Sharks stop listening to the entrepreneurs and say, "I'm out."

"Great leaders are great listeners."

Listening is a key to success. I think that great leaders are great listeners and think of it as both a skill and an art. Of course, as a leader you ultimately have to make the decision about what makes sense and what does not, but you can't make an informed decision if you don't listen.

Dave Kerpen is CEO and co-founder of a social media agency, Likeable, and author of the book, *Likeable Social Media*, which made the "New York Times" best seller list. In an article Kerpen wrote for an American Express online business forum, he stated that, of all the skills a CEO needs to succeed, listening is probably the most valuable, and yet, the most underrated.[10]

Kerpen said that listening to your team is the first step to meeting their needs and helping them to feel valued. It's human nature to want to feel heard, so fostering that in your organization will motivate people to perform to the best of their ability. It will also help to shape and improve your company culture, which is extremely important these days.

Listening also means paying attention to what is going on in your market, in your community, and in the world. I read the "Wall Street Journal," tune into the news on TV, and look at other newspapers and online information sources. I can't just limit my awareness to business issues because you cannot be innovative if you're just focused on your business; you have to pay attention to all the moving parts within your life as a whole.

In order to be successful in business, you need to be creative in your thinking and approach. You need to be able to roll with the punches and navigate the ups and downs that come with being a business owner. I have found that this necessary creativity

---

10. "Why the best CEOs listen more," Dave Kerpen.
www.americanexpress.com/us/small-business/openforum/articles/the-kpis-of-listening-for-ceos/

comes when you're not actively seeking it. It's often in those moments of relaxation or rest that those great ideas and solutions come.

Additionally, you cannot succeed if you don't have a support system and outlets outside of work. These elements of your life not only make you feel more fulfilled, but they also strengthen your mindset. Developing and fostering your relationships has a fantastic side effect — it develops your emotional intelligence and maturity. This helps you to truly understand other points of view. This empathy will make you a more effective business partner and employer. For example, it gave me the ability to recognize both the clear stars in my organization, *and* the low performers who have the ability to become stars given the right support.

While I understand and listen to other points of view, I choose not to listen to naysayers. At least, not entirely. I'll turn up the volume for a second to hear the useful nuggets of information they have to share; then I tune out the rest by turning the volume back down.

Chapter 10
That Vision Thing

As a business owner, you must create a well-written mission statement and vision statement. A mission statement is a definition of your organization at present, what it does, and why it exists. The vision statement is usually focused on the future, on what your business wants to do, and where it is headed. Your mission statement and vision statement are the forces that drive your organization; they are intended to motivate you and your employees and remind everyone of the overall focus of your business.

Your vision statement and mission statement are declarations that show how your business is about something bigger than yourself — that you are working toward something beyond yourself and beyond just making money.

For example, Nike® is known for the business motto: *"Just do it."* The Nike® mission statement is also short and sweet: (*To*) *"bring inspiration and innovation to every athlete* in the world."* (If you follow the asterisk, it leads to the statement: *"If you have a body, you are an athlete."*)

Starbucks says: *"Our mission: to inspire and nurture the human spirit—one person, one cup, and one neighborhood at a time."*

Facebook's mission statement used to be: *"Facebook helps you connect and share with the people in your life."* That mission statement evolved *into "Facebook's mission is to give people the power to share and make the world more open and connected."*

Did you notice that none of those companies said their mission is to make a whole bunch of money, even if that is exactly what they are doing?

MZM's vision statement: *By constantly learning and adapting in order to improve our deliverables through construction and transportation, MZM will be the best company in the region, providing our full suite of services beyond the expected standards, for our clients and employees.*

Our mission statement: *To be customer-driven and profit-focused, by providing quality services, which will ensure a strong sustainable foundation for our continued success and that of our clients and employees.*

You will of course, need to develop a good business plan. Your vision of who you are as a company, and your mission statement's reflection of what you do, must be part of your business plan. Let the care you give to drafting these statements be a reflection of the care and attention you will give to running your business.

Why is it so important to have a vision statement and a mission statement? Because you need to think about what you are doing, why you went into business, and whom you serve. Your reasons cannot just be about chasing money. I went into business to build wealth and I have no problem with that. But if that is your *only* goal, then what happens if you don't make any money by the end of the year? Where does that leave you? In fact, a lot of people who have made money their only motivation have wound up in jail. Principles and integrity count in life and in business. What you stand for will attract people to you and to your organization.

Additionally, without a mission and vision statement, it is unlikely any bank or investor will talk to you. You need to define the goals you are striving toward and create a mission statement that inspires all who read it.

Your mission and vision may evolve, just as Facebook's did. A 2009 article in the "New York Observer" looked at the evolution of Facebook's mission statement, noting: "No longer for merely posting pictures of drunk people from the holiday party, Facebook now empowers users to change the world by posting links, connecting with other influencers, sharing stories, and donating and buying products."[11]

Like Facebook, you should update your mission and vision statements in the same way someone would update a resume. Is your business really the same creature today as it was when you started it?

Your mission and vision statements are not just a bunch of words. They are a reflection of what keeps you, the small business owner, going when things get tough. They are the clear, specific guidelines and values that you will follow on your journey to success. They define and differentiate you from your competitors.

You should write what you believe.

---

11. "The evolution of Facebook's Mission Statement."
observer.com/2009/07/the-evolution-of-facebooks-mission-statement/

Chapter 11

Anyone Who Has a Business Needs a Business Plan

These days, most people refer to a business plan as a "growth plan," and so will I. Your plan is a document which provides a clear look at your business. It answers the questions:

- What do you do?
- How do you do it?
- What are the strategies you've formed to grow your business?
- What metrics will you use to prove that your ideas are valid?
- Who are your customers?
- How are you going to get more of them?
- Who are your competitors?
- How are you going to succeed in spite of them?
- What are your financial numbers: debts, sales, profits, liabilities?

Having this information shows that you know what you're doing. Your business plan is necessary if you want to convince anyone who doesn't love you like your mother does to think about investing so much as a dime in your organization.

You can't go to any bank or investor without a well-developed growth plan. If you would like to write a good growth plan, you can find plenty of help at local colleges, municipal business offices, Small Business Administration affiliates, and public agencies. Even if you're not immediately looking for loans or investors, formulating a growth plan can help you better understand your business. Compiling a growth plan compels you to confront the weaknesses in your business and study its strengths. It forces you to think about the future and how to get there. There is no better way to tell if what you think is a beauty mark is really a wart.

As John Warrilow wrote in his book, *Built to Sell*, everyone should build a business as if they plan to sell it in the future. This means making your business marketable and scalable so that it may one day be valuable to someone other than yourself. This strategy will enable you to stay in scalable conversations and fortify your organization so that it lasts.

The major mistake many owners make is to plan from only their perspective. They think their great idea is the most important thing and that it is *so* great, it just can't fail. Of course, it can and they need to prove why it won't. If they forget about their customers, who they are, and how to get them, they will inevitably collapse. The cupcake maker says, "I'll grow because everybody likes cupcakes," with no thought about the five other bakeries within four blocks that they need to differentiate from.

A fellow NJ-based business consultant and growth expert, Carl Gould, has said that business owners tend to "Fall in love with their product instead of with their customer." In other words, they get so attached to what they're offering, they forget about who they're offering it *to*. Remember this: a great idea that isn't sellable is not actually a great idea. Focus on the problem you're solving or value you're offering to your customers instead of just the features of your product or service.

I teach at the New Jersey Institute of Technology in Newark, and my students have to create a theoretical growth plan as part of the class. Here are some common mistakes they tend to make, just as many business owners do:

One team of students wrote a growth plan for a winery. One of their goals was to start donating to a charity as soon as they opened their doors. Philanthropy is good, but the time, energy, and money you spend on an overly ambitious charitable program might be better applied to building your business when your business is in that tricky startup phase. Concentrate on everything that you need to put in place to make your business successful first, *then* you can give back.

Another group of students had an idea for a mobile drycleaner. They handed in 40 pages of fluff in which they basically repeated the same information they'd shared in the first four pages. They didn't include the details to explain the "how" and "why" of what they planned to do.

Now, the wine group also created a video presentation, brought in wine samples, the works. Is all of that necessary if you're making a presentation to investors? It depends on your business. What you must do is capture the investors' interest and attention in those first 30 or 40 seconds. That means you have less than a minute to make those who are listening or reading want more. What they want to hear is how you expect to make money. In other words, they want to know how you expect to first repay their investment, and then earn them even more money down the line.

No fancy presentation will ever cover for you if you can't answer their money questions. For example: *How will this loan take your business to the next level?* That's what investors and banks want to know.

However, you need to know that few banks or investors are interested in funding startups. They typically look for businesses with a track record of at least two to three years. If you've been in business for that length of time, your growth plan and presentation must convince them that what you've been doing works, and that what you plan to do makes sense.

Get help writing your growth plan. You can see samples and elicit advice from the Small Business Administration and other sources.[12] Invest in coaching to learn how to make a presentation to an investor or loan officer at your bank. Getting this kind of help is not just a good idea; it is essential.

12. US Small Business Administration: "Create Your Business Plan." www.sba.gov/writing-business-plan

Chapter 12

Why Are You in the Same Place?

Why isn't your business moving up to the next level?

As I mentioned much earlier, if you've had the same number of clients and the same amount of business or revenue over the years, and you are content with where you are, then what you really want is reliable income. This kind of complacency equates to a "job mentality" and says that expansion for economic growth is not really on your radar. People who don't take risks, hustle, network, or strategize will remain stagnant.

Business is like marriage; if you don't keep it stimulated, it is going to stagnate or die. People who take the "job mentality" approach to their marriages are called "soon-to-be-divorced."

Stagnation is not a good thing in any human endeavor: not in marriage, and not in business. You may be content with the status quo, but that trusty handful of customers could die or disappear. They could start doing business with your competitors, who are hungrier and more energetic than you are. There is always someone else coming along, someone who could push you out and put an end to your comfy "paycheck." As small as your business may be, you've got to keep it growing to keep it going.

Remember the little mom and pop bookstores that were supplanted by the big chain mega bookstores? At first, only the mom-and-pop stores disappeared. Then, as things continued to shift, the large chain stores began to disappear because of online book dealing. Now, a small group of people still invest in physical books, but they've almost become a novelty with the rise of e-books and audio books.

Here are some questions to help you refresh your business:

- Are you currently using technology to support your business?
- Do you have a website?
- Is that website interactive or static?
- Does your website meet the current standards for mobile friendliness?
- Is your website exactly the same today as when you launched it a couple of years ago?
- Are you using social media to market your business?
- Do you know what your competition is up to?
- Do you encourage your employees to identify problems and suggest solutions?
- Do you seek out customer feedback?
- Do you assume that if no one is complaining everything is fine?

In the spring of 2014, I was accepted into the Goldman Sachs 10,000 Small Businesses education program. The investment firm had committed $500 million to help small businesses create jobs and economic opportunity, as well as receive greater access to support services, such as business education.

The Goldman Sachs program taught superb classes on negotiations and leadership styles. They also forced me to spend a significant amount of time (thirteen eight-hour sessions every other week) thinking about my business and how to make it grow — not just about doing the deals and getting the work done. During this structured time, my only task was to think about my financial ratios, my growth strategy, and my succession plan.

One insight I had from the sessions was the realization that I was further along than I'd originally thought. I left some of the classes thinking, *"Marge Perry, you're doing pretty good."* I'd been there, done that, and learned a lot of what the course covered, albeit the hard way in some cases.

I left the program with an updated, elevated version of my existing growth plan and a better sense of how to take my business to the next level. I recommend it — it is a good program for any small business.

Continuous education — both formal and informal — is a must. Accept the fact that whatever you were doing five years ago is probably becoming irrelevant and you need to reevaluate your strategy to ensure it isn't obsolete. Your mindset has to expand along with your business, so you must be constantly looking to learn, or even unlearn some of the things that you've been doing that no longer make sense.

Your business will not survive if you don't do this. I don't know anyone who has been successful in business for any period of time who does not invest the time to ensure that they are at the top of their game. This also means upskilling your employees whenever possible and realistic.

You must be hungry for knowledge, and you need to learn how to transfer that knowledge back into your business. Examine the weaknesses in yourself and in your business and seek guidance and knowledge in those areas. For example, I told you how much I hate to fire people, so I brought on a fractional HR professional to help me do a better job of hiring.

Even if you're successful and making money, you cannot ignore what's not working. It will catch up to you eventually. If you don't know how to fix it, take a class. There are many options available at universities and junior colleges which can teach you everything from reading a financial statement to improving your business plan.

I've taken courses at universities and even attended classes offered by New Jersey Transit and the Port Authority of New York and New Jersey. Those are public entities that look to educate small businesses, particularly for minority and women-owned companies. Their goal is to create more enterprises that are prepared to bid on the contracts that these entities offer. Taking the course does not guarantee that we will get the work; it means we are better prepared to bid. This put us in a much better position to go after a contract.

You can also find additional learning opportunities from your peers — your fellow business owners. Organizations like SCORE and other Small Business Development Centers (SBCDs) can help give you guidance and put the whole journey into perspective. The people you meet here can reassure you about the growing pains of developing as a business owner, talk through your challenges with you, and provide support and education at the same time.

Seek knowledge out and you will find learning opportunities in your community.

Remember when I took that $1 million loss? I was still ignorant about so much. Please learn from my mistakes, so you don't have to repeat them. In my case, I went back to school and earned my Masters in Business Administration from the New Jersey Institute of Technology. I also attended classes at Dartmouth College and took their "Leadership for the 21st Century" course at the Tuck School of Business.

"Anything that moves you forward also moves your business forward."

Putting yourself in new learning environments may take time away from you being able to work in your business, but the knowledge you will gain as a result will be invaluable. Knowledge is more powerful today than ever before; it is the fuel that propels enterprise. You are your business, so anything that moves you forward also moves your business forward.

Year by year, look at your business's growth and ask whether you made the numbers you projected. If not, ask why you missed. If you are not seeing the growth you projected, check in with your advisory team. You might also think about hiring a business coach or going back to school. Most professionals are required to get some kind of continuing education to stay current in their field, so require it of yourself.

Remember, your "job" is to work *on* the business not just *in* the business. Getting bogged down in the little details instead of working on the big picture will keep your business small, tight, and limited. If you remember to take a step back, you can see the entire garden you're growing, not just the individual sprouts. That way, you'll know which plants to water and where to plant more, then watch it all flourish.

Chapter 13

Giving Back

I know, I know...I said it was a mistake for the students mapping out a startup business plan to include a big-time charitable component from day one. But once established, your business should be giving to the community in the form of money, your time, or your talent.

For years, I would assemble my team for monthly service, such as helping build Habitat for Humanity houses. During this time, money was tight for MZM, but I talked the guys into contributing volunteer work. For us, it was also a teambuilding exercise and a morale booster. There was a job that needed to be done and my crew could do it well. We once helped build a homeless shelter in Newark, and I continue offering my construction services for similar causes.

I also decided to start a scholarship fund. In the beginning, I was able to offer a $500 college scholarship, and as my business grew, I've now come close to offering $15,000 a year, split between my undergraduate and graduate alma maters: Kean University in Union, New Jersey and the New Jersey Institute of Technology in Newark.

Additionally, I offer my time to sit on panels and contribute to the forums that provide new entrepreneurs and business owners with advice. I participate in programs to motivate students, press for diversity, and bring light to women's issues and other causes I care about.

I serve as a mentor, just as others have served me, so that I can provide advice to those who are starting up their own enterprises. Giving back is one of the primary reasons I'm writing this book — so that *you* can build your business with success.

If someone asks me, *"Why should I give anything? What's in it for me?"* I find it hard to continue in the conversation. Yes, giving is good for publicity, marketing, and recruitment. The experts will tell you that when you sponsor something, people in your community see you in a positive light, and there is a business benefit to that. Potential customers may like to do business with those who play an active part in the community and people feel good about working at a company with a charitable reputation. Your giving might even attract the kind of star employee a small company would otherwise lose to a big corporation. Experts agree that giving your time and money reaps brand recognition.

But to me, giving is not about getting a payback. I don't know anyone in business who has not benefited from someone offering them advice, encouragement, a hand up, or a shoulder to cry on. I hesitate to start naming those who helped me because the list is long, and I would not want to leave anyone out. Where would any of us be if others had not reached back in some way to lift us up? You should want to pay it back and pay it forward.

In addition, businesses are a special type of citizen. Through our charity and our participation, our businesses bring others to the table for a cause. We can, through our involvement, make others see that some unmet need matters and must be addressed. We can help change the world.

Chapter 14

Taking Care of Business Means Taking Care of Yourself

Water inspires me and relaxes me. I like to sit in a rocking chair by the beach and just watch the water. Sometimes I'll think about a problem I need to solve and work it out in my mind, looking for inspiration in the rhythm of the waves. Many times, I just let the inner noise fade until my mind goes quiet.

In the hustle and bustle of your daily business activities, you have to remember to take care of yourself. You have to allow yourself some down time away from your business. If you want to take care of your business, you must take care of yourself and keep the personal you and professional you in balance.

Most importantly, you've got to believe that you are deserving of self-care. When my crisis hit and I lost all that money, I stopped feeling that I was worthy of that care. I was in so deep, I made the mistake of forgetting to still love myself.

When you get into trouble, the first thing you sacrifice is taking the time to nurture yourself. That entrepreneur mode kicks in, and you go into overdrive, refusing to admit defeat, or stop until you're out of danger. The adrenaline surges the way it does when someone instantly summons the strength to lift a vehicle off of a victim of a car accident; all of your attention and energy goes to lifting the crisis off of your business.

In my case, I was convinced that there was no money or time available for self-care. The IRS or the banks were going to shut me down, so there was certainly no time or money available for a vacation.

This was yet another mistake. Looking back, I wish I had dedicated more time to taking care of myself. You burn out and lose your creativity when you don't allow yourself the time and space to properly rest and recover. The hard truth is, if you are falling apart, so is your business. You can't steer the ship properly if you're too exhausted to see straight.

So it is okay — **and** sometimes absolutely necessary — to take a step back and say, "I love you, business. But at the end of the day, I love *me* more."

If you can't take a long vacation, that's okay. Take a walk around the local park for fifteen minutes. Have lunch with a friend and talk about anything other than work. Read a couple chapters of a novel. Browse around a nice store, even if you don't buy anything. (You have the willpower. You can do it.) Do *something* you love that allows you to take an hour for yourself. It may not seem like a lot, but it can make all the difference in the world.

Whether you are a business owner who is single, a business owner who is married, or if you are married to both your partner and a business that you run together, your relationship can influence your business's failure or success, and your business can affect your relationship's failure or success. Again, balance is the key.

Take me, for example: I'm not married, and I don't have kids even though I have always wanted both. Some people will be tempted to blame my being single on my business, but they'd be incorrect since I didn't start my own business until I was in my 40's. There was plenty of time for me to have gotten married before that, but I didn't. I always had a boyfriend; that wasn't the problem. I am just not one of those women who must have a man or a ring on my finger. For a time, I was attracted to younger guys, but it turned out they were more attracted to my money than they were to me, so I decided it was time to stop and do nothing in the dating arena for a while.

Now, I've discovered that I am completely comfortable in my own skin. I embrace my singlehood. I have a wonderful group of friends that I hang out with, and I am happy and at peace. I don't have to be tied to anyone else to experience real enjoyment and fulfilment because there is always "wonderful Marjorie" to hang out with. I have given myself the gift of falling madly in love with myself, and I'm good with that. Marriage? Maybe it will happen. But what I truly want is to have the right person, who enhances my life as I continue to bring my business to new heights.

And what about you? If you are a woman business owner, it's pretty much guaranteed that you are making sacrifices. Certainly, the men do, too. We all spend an incredible number of hours working and devoting ourselves to what we do. But it is still much more common for a man to have a partner at home, taking care of the children (if they have them) and handling the domestic labor. This is still less common for women.

Traditionally, women often have to handle the responsibilities of home and family even if both partners are working. If you are a woman business owner, what can you do to create more balance?

According to the research conducted by a consultancy firm called Womenable, the number of businesses in the United States increased by 47 percent from 1977-2014. However, the number of women-owned enterprises increased by a whopping 68 percent. That percentage is one-and-a-half times the number for all businesses.[13] Additionally, revenues for women-owned companies went up 72 percent. Only the largest, publicly traded firms racked up a higher growth.

The data shows that women business owners can, and do, hold their own. (But we already knew that didn't we?) There is still a lot of work to do in order to remove existing roadblocks and empower women to grow their businesses even further.

It's okay and necessary to work hard, but remember, if you want to create growth in your business, you've got to practice self-care as you juggle all of your personal responsibilities and build momentum in your business.

Can a woman be a successful entrepreneur and be married? It depends on the marriage. You have to marry the right partner. You have to marry someone who understands and supports your dreams. If you are like me and you get up at three in the morning when a project is due and come home late at night, who will feed your children and get them ready for school? You need a partner who is going to work with you to handle everything that needs to be done to keep your family healthy and thriving.

And men, you have to learn how to balance your time, too. Don't miss all the football games and soccer games you used to love or stop spending time with your spouse because you can't pull yourself away from your business.

---

13. "The 2014 State of Women-Owned Businesses Report: A Summary of Important Trends, 1997-2014."

Womenable.com https://nawbo.org/sites/nawbo/files/2014_state_of_women-owned_businesses.pdf

Divorce can be a very real threat, particularly in the first two or three years of a business, because in those years, you are giving your lifeblood to your business.

What if you are a couple working together in your business? Working with a spouse can be fantastic if the two of you take on complementary roles and are truly equals in what you do. This takes excellent communication and a well-concerted effort to separate your working and personal relationships.

Even in the best of such situations, I highly suggest that you create timeouts from your business lives together, so that when you come home, your conversation revolves around something that has nothing to do with your work. There has to be a time when one of you says, *"Let's get away for the weekend, no business, just us."* Otherwise, being in business together can destroy the precious intimacy in your relationship.

No matter your relationship status, I support you in creating a life in which your business grows, the people in your life matter, and you matter. I applaud you for doing what you need to do to create a life of balance, joy, and financial success as you take the necessary steps to build your business.

Epilogue

When I look forward and think about the future, I feel good.

My business is strong and has continued to work on big projects, such as the new Terminal A at Newark Liberty International Airport. I have learned many lessons over the years, and I continue to become a savvier businesswoman with a clearer picture of what lies ahead. I am confident in what I do and how I do it, and I am ironclad in my integrity and my convictions. That comes through in my daily operations and is clear to everyone who works with me. Because of this, I know that great things are in the future for MZM.

Another part of what is important to me now is that I speak at conferences and meetings where I can tell people who are thinking about going into business, "*You can do it!*" It takes hard work, good planning, and a commitment. You can't fool yourself. You have to be realistic, but you can do it.

I want to encourage others as I am encouraging you. That's why I teach a course at the New Jersey Institute of Technology, why I mentor others independently, and why I provide scholarships.

You know, I didn't always believe that I was powerful. The truth is, I *am* powerful, and so are you. Those of us who engage in commerce and who provide services and jobs, we are powerful.

I have been tested in life, as I'm sure you have, too. Whatever I go through, I have to make sure that I am standing in my power and in my love.

The true "me" is extremely strong, extremely compassionate, extremely giving, extremely kind, extremely crazy, and all over the place at times. And the true "me" is of service to God.

There were times when I thought I was the biblical Job. But the true "me" now trusts and believes. And the true "me" doesn't make excuses.

I persevere, and I get the job done.

Now, show me how you do it.

Acknowledgments

Many thanks to my writer and publicist Barry Cohen—the best, who kept me on schedule. Thank you to Nicole Herviou for great edits and rewrites, and to Hurley Fox of *Fox and Friends* for his guidance support.

About the Author

Marjorie Perry, a lifelong resident of New Jersey, is the President and CEO of MZM Construction & Management Company, Inc. Equally as important, she is widely recognized as an innovator, public speaker, writer, and role model for women and minorities in business. Using her extraordinary path to success and 26 years of experience as fodder for inspiration, Perry finds her mission to be one who motivates nascent entrepreneurs to develop and pursue their dreams by sharing the lessons she has learned from her own success, which often meant taking life's lemons and making lemonade. Trained as an educator with a B.A. from Kean College, Perry's path in teaching was diverted after she was caught in a series of layoffs in the Newark Public School system. In a fortuitous career move, she decided to try her luck in sales and marketing — which turned out to be an unexpected perfect fit. She went on to work for corporate giants 3M, Johnson & Johnson, and United Airlines, ultimately cultivating a burgeoning vision for life as a passionate, self-made entrepreneur.

Perry launched a consulting company focused on helping start-ups and serial entrepreneurs succeed in the marketplace.

Resourceful and open to all possibilities, it wasn't long before she and two partners founded MZM Construction & Management. Soon after, she became sole principal of the company, which has sustained a multi-million-dollar bottom line for the last 24 years.

Perry is now a coveted inspirational speaker and writer, motivating people with the message that, "You, too, can do it!" She has spoken throughout the United States to women in business and at small business conferences on how to successfully navigate while playing in shark-filled waters.

Speaking engagements include the NJ Governor's Conference for Women, the heralded Sobel & Co., Executive Women Breakfast Series, The Liberty Science Women's Program, The National Association of Women Business Owners, The NJ chapter of Financial Executive Institute (FEI), Columbia Bank, Berkeley College, Goldman Sacks, City of Pittsburgh, City of Cincinnati, City of Newark Women in Construction NYU, Morristown Chamber of Commerce, NJBIA, Ted Talk, and Women in Business Miami Florida.

Perry has appeared on MSNBC, CBS, ABC, UPN 9, News 12, and NJN's New Jersey Caucus with Steve Adubato where she also is a proud member of the Adubato Advisory Board.

She has received numerous awards and recognitions, including being inducted into New Jersey's premier business publication's NJBIZ 2011 Business of the Year, New Jersey Business Hall of Fame, 2012 SBA Business of the Year, and 2012 Best 50 Women in Business. She has also been named one of the Top 25 Entrepreneurs in New Jersey. Perry was also elected by Goldman Sachs and Bloomberg in 2015 as one of the top 15 businesses in the country to watch for in the future with major growth within the next five years. To top it off, she has been selected to receive the prestigious 2018 NJBIZ Lifetime Achievement Award, which has only been presented to three other New Jersey businesswomen over the years.

Perry sits on the following boards: The Board of Directors Chair Emeritus and Finance Chair at NJIT, Harvard University Advisory Board, RWJ UMDNJ Board of Trustees, the Newark Regional Business Partnership, and the M&T Bank and African American Chamber. She is a prior Board member of the Montclair State University Feliciano Center for Entrepreneurship, New Jersey Chamber of Commerce Secretary and Executive Committee, and Kean University and Business School. She served two terms as the Finance Chair for the East Orange School Board and is a past member of the New Jersey Economic Development Authority and Kean University Foundation Board. In academia, she was an adjunct professor at NJIT and Stevens Institute of Technology from 2015 to 2018, teaching MBA students the means and methods of best practices to be successful entrepreneurs. In her spare time, Perry mentors inner city college-bound youth because it matters that they make it too.

Perry excelled in receiving her MBA from NJIT with credited course work in civil engineering; she did additional coursework at Rutgers, Stevens, NYU, and NJIT and completed Leadership for the 21st Century at the Tuck School of Business at Dartmouth College. In addition, she completed a finance certification program in 2016 from Dartmouth. She graduated Harvard Business School (HBS) OPM Executive Program and was voted class speaker in November of 2020. Finally, Perry is proud to have been a constructor on the new Terminal A Newark Port Authority NY/NJ.

You can find out more at https://www.marjorieaperry.com/.

About MZM

MZM Construction & Management Company is a full-service construction management and transportation company serving a wide variety of clients, including small businesses, Fortune 500 companies, government agencies, nonprofits, educational institutions, and many others. MZM has more than 20 years of construction management experience and has developed a reputation for completing quality projects on time and on budget for its clients. MZM is certified to handle solid waste disposal in several states, serving the needs of clients with its own fleet of trucks. Additionally, MZM provides customized transportation programs tailored to the needs of each client. You can learn more at www.mzmcc.com.

For sales, editorial information, subsidiary rights information or a catalog, please write or phone or e-mail,

Brick Tower Press
Manhanset House
Shelter Island Hts., New York 11965-0342, US
Tel: 212-427-7139
www.BrickTowerPress.com
bricktower@aol.com
www.IngramContent.com

For sales in the UK and Europe please contact our distributor,

Gazelle Book Services
White Cross Mills
Lancaster, LA1 4XS, UK
Tel: (01524) 68765 Fax: (01524) 63232
email: jacky@gazellebooks.co.uk